Cooking

WITH BEER

Favourites of Newfoundland & Labrador

Gerry Crewe

Cooking

WITH BEER

Favourites of Newfoundland & Labrador

Gerry Crewe

CREATIVE PUBLISHERS

St. John's, Newfoundland and Labrador
2008

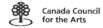

Canada Council　Conseil des Arts
for the Arts　　du Canada

Newfoundland
Labrador

We gratefully acknowledge the financial support of the Canada Council for the Arts, the Government of Canada through the Book Publishing Industry Development Program (BPIDP), and the Government of Newfoundland and Labrador through the Department of Tourism, Culture and Recreation for our publishing program.

Cover Design and Photos by Maurice Fitzgerald
Layout by Joanne Snook-Hann
Printed on acid-free paper

Published by
CREATIVE PUBLISHERS
an imprint of CREATIVE BOOK PUBLISHING
a Transcontinental Inc. associated company
P.O. Box 8660, Stn. A
St. John's, Newfoundland and Labrador A1B 3T7

Printed in Canada by:
TRANSCONTINENTAL INC.

Library and Archives Canada Cataloguing in Publication

Crewe, Gerry, 1948-
　　Cooking with beer : Newfoundland favourites / Gerry Crewe.

ISBN 978-1-897174-26-5

　　1. Cookery (Beer). I. Title.

TX726.3.C74 2008　　　　　641.6'23　　　　　C2008-900309-8

*This book is dedicated to my sister, Eileen (Crewe) Moore,
who was a major influence on my career.*

GERRY CREWE was born and educated in St. John's. He started in the food business at the Hotel Newfoundland in 1965. Over the past thirty-four and a half years Gerry has worked throughout Canada and the United States. He has been a chef instructor in the culinary arts and was a founding member of the Newfoundland and Labrador Chefs Association, of which he was president for the past six years. He is a four-time winner of Chef of the Year in Newfoundland and a two-time winner of the Atlantic Chef of the Year. He won the Teaching Award of Excellence, provincially. As well he was part of Team Canada at the World Cooks Tour of Africa and also in Ireland. He is presently retired.

A History of Quidi Vidi Brewery

FOUNDED BY David Rees and David Fong, the brewery competes in a market which has been dominated by national and international giants.

There are a number of things that set this local brewery apart from the national breweries. Unlike the nationals, the design and location of the plant are deeply connected to the local roots of its founders. The newly reconstructed building, formerly the Cabot Seafood's Plant, sits surrounded by granite cliffs at the mouth of the harbour in Quidi Vidi Village. With its green spruce clapboard and white trim, it looks comfortably at home within the rustic surroundings of the village. This ultra-modern facility houses a state-of-the-art brewery, a retail store, administrative offices, and reception room.

Prior to start-up in 1996, Dave & Dave (both engineers in the offshore oil industry) had been assessing potential manufacturing opportunities in Newfoundland and Labrador. Their objectives were simple. They wanted to develop an enterprise that was new to the province, but more importantly, one that would create new jobs for the province, rather than simply replace existing ones.

Through their involvement in the offshore, they had traveled extensively throughout North America and had noticed an

upsurge in brewing activity across the continent. Not only were breweries on the increase, the beers they were producing were being embraced by a consuming public who had seemingly grown tired of the non-descript beer styles being produced by the larger breweries. Realizing that no such enterprise existed in the province at that time, they commissioned the development of a feasibility study to assess the potential of such an enterprise in Newfoundland and Labrador.

The first beer hit the market in August of 1996, then in the winter of 1997, they came out with the Northern Light and the Hibernia Lager (this one was to celebrate the towout of the Hibernia platform).

They came out with the Honey Brown and Honey Brown Light later. In 2000, they launched the Erics Red for the Viking celebrations and it has stayed with them to this day. In 2001, they entered the Eric's Brand in the Chicago World Beer Championships and placed second in that Global competition.

Two years ago, Quidi Vidi Brewery launched their first mainstream beer brands, the QV and QV Light, to give Newfoundland a product similar to the kind of beer they like to drink.

The most recent addition is a type of beer called Cranberry Cloud. It is made to compete in the cooler market more than the beer market.

Quidi Vidi has become a destination for visitors to our province. They have offered tours over the years and that part of the business continues to grow. As an extension to that, they are in the process of preparing for next season by making improvements to the hospitality room so visitors can have pub snacks for lunch.

They currently sell their beer in Nova Scotia, and are attempting to get it in Alberta. Another possibility is that it could be back to Iceland soon.

Table of Contents

Appetizers

Curried Beer Puffs

1 clove garlic, minced
4 oz. minced onion
1 tbsp. salad oil
2 tbsp. butter
2 tbsp. flour
2 oz. milk
4 oz. QV Light beer
8 oz. lean ground beef
½ tsp. salt
1 tbsp. curry powder

Brown meat in 350°F oven for 7 to 8 minutes and set aside.

Sauté the onion and garlic in oil for about 5 minutes.

Add the ground beef (cooked).

Add the curry powder.

Make a roux; in other words, melt the butter in a saucepan, stir in the flour and cook for about 2 minutes, stirring constantly.

Add the milk and beer, cook over low heat and slowly bring to a boil.

Cook for 3 to 5 minutes.

Add the meat mixture.

Season.

Let cool and fill puffs.

Puffs

2 oz. butter
8 oz. all purpose flour
Dash salt
4 eggs
8 oz. QV Light beer

Preheat oven to 450°F.

Bring the beer to a boil. Add the butter and melt.

Add the flour and salt.

Stir and cook until the mixture comes free from the pot and forms a ball.

Remove from heat and cool.

When cool, add 1 egg at a time and beat well.

Drop by a teaspoon or use a pastry bag about the size of a loonie.

Bake on a buttered baking dish or parchment paper.

Bake 10 minutes at 450°F.

Reduce heat to 350°F and bake for another 10 minutes.

Cool. Split and fill with curried mixture.

Makes about 3 dozen.

Chef's Hint
*When removing from oven, put puffs on a cake rack,
as leaving them on a cookie sheet they may become soggy.*

QV Bruschetta

Baguette
2 oz. onions, sliced thin
2 oz. chicken stock
2 oz. QV Light beer
1 oz. parmesan cheese, grated
1 oz. sundried tomatoes
1 oz. parsley, chopped
1 tsp. balsamic vinegar
1 tsp. olive oil
Pinch of fresh garlic, minced
Salt and pepper to taste

Combine chicken stock, beer, sundried tomatoes and onions in a sauté pan.

Bring to a boil.

Simmer for about 20 minutes until 2 teaspoons of liquid remains.

Add half the parmesan cheese, vinegar and parsley.

Salt and pepper to taste.

Cut baguette into desired thickness.

Put on cookie sheet and brush with the oil and garlic combination.

Toast in a hot oven.

Cover the toasted baguette with the tomato and onion mixture.

Sprinkle with parmesan cheese.

Put in hot oven until cheese melts.

Calamari - Beer Battered

2½ lbs. squid
1½ cups rye flour
1 tbsp. vegetable oil
24 oz. QV Light beer
5 egg whites, well beaten
Salt and pepper to taste

Using the chart in this book, clean the squid, reserving the bodies.

Wash the interior of the body with cold water.

Dry with paper towels.

Combine flour, oil, salt and pepper in a bowl.

Whisk to mix well.

Slowly add the beer, a little at a time.

Fold in egg whites (be careful).

Cut squid body into half inch rings.

Heat deep fryer to 350°F.

Dip into batter and fry for a couple of minutes until golden brown.

Serve hot.

Chef's Hint

Try one ring and if batter comes off during cooking, dust squid with flour.
Put on a cake rack to drain excess grease.

Ham and Beer Meatballs

8 oz. ham, finely ground
16 oz. lean pork, finely ground
1 cup sourdough breadcrumbs
3 tbsp. milk
2 tbsp. dill, finely chopped
½ tsp. caraway seeds
4 oz. green onions, finely chopped
2 tbsp. margarine
1 tbsp. Dijon mustard
2 cloves garlic, minced
4 tbsp. parsley, finely chopped
1 egg
2 tbsp. vegetable oil
6 oz. Honey Light beer
Salt and pepper to taste

Soak the crumbs in milk for 5 minutes.

Mix together the meats, soaked crumbs, seasoning, egg and mustard; mix thoroughly.

Form into balls and chill.

Melt margarine and oil together.

When hot, add the meatballs and toss them until all are coated.

Transfer the meatball to a baking dish.

Bake at 400°F for about 5 minutes.

Add the beer to the pan and reduce to half.

Pour beer mixture over meatballs.

Cover tightly with foil.

Lower temperature to 350°F and bake until tender.

Note: Serve immediately.

Meatballs and Beer

24 oz. lean ground beef
4 oz. QV beer
4 oz. chili sauce
1 tsp. Worcestershire sauce
1 tsp. sugar
2 tsp. salt
Dash pepper
Dash Tabasco sauce
3 tbsp. water

Mix together the beef, 1 teaspoon of salt and water.

Shape into balls.

Brown the meatballs in the butter.

Mix the beer, chili sauce, Worcestershire sauce, sugar, Tabasco sauce, and the remaining salt and pepper.

Pour over the meatballs.

Finish in a preheated 350°F oven for approximately 7 to 8 minutes.

Serve with toothpicks.

Note: Serve immediately.

QV Beer Bread

12 oz. QV beer, bring to a boil
½ cup lukewarm water
1 tbsp. sugar
1½ tbsp. shortening
4 cups all purpose flour
2 tsp. salt
1 package or envelope of active dry yeast
1 beaten egg white
1 tsp. sugar

Add shortening and sugar to hot beer.

Stir until it is dissolved.

Cool to lukewarm.

Add yeast to bowl and gently pour lukewarm water plus sugar over it.

Combine beer, shortening, sugar mixture with yeast and water sugar mixture.

Stir all purpose flour and salt together in a large bowl.

Make a well in the centre.

Add the liquids.

Mix thoroughly.

Put into a large, slightly greased bowl.

Brush top with metal margarine.

Cover with plastic wrap, loosely, or a damp cloth.

Let proof (rise) in a warm place for approximately 2 hours.

Punch down dough.

Shape into desired shapes (rolls or bread).

Put in greased pans.

Brush tops with melted margarine (slightly).

Set to rise uncovered in a warm place.

When double in size, place in a 350° F oven until golden brown.

Remove from oven and place on a bread rack. Brush lightly with melted margarine.

Chefs Hints

If using a board, dust with flour before punching dough, or it may stick.

If using a rolling pin to roll out dough, also dust with flour.

When bread is removed from the oven and out of the pans, tap the bottom of the loaf and you should get a hollow sound.

*If there is a soft crust on bread or rolls,
grease the top after taking from the oven.*

***Note:** Beer is not used very often in the making of breads.
It imparts a pleasant, sourish flavour and a lightness of texture.
The carbon dioxide in the beer lightens the dough and it is faster
rising. It is very important to always use freshly opened beer
bottles or cans, unless the recipe calls for flat beer.*

QV Light Cheese Spreads

1 cup grated cheddar or marble cheese
1 tsp. minced green onion
2 tbsp. margarine or butter
2 tbsp. QV Light beer
1 tsp. Dijon mustard
Pinch of cayenne pepper, anchovy paste and caraway seeds

Mix all the ingredients together in a bowl, except for beer.

When all is mixed, add and mix the beer.

Clam and 1892 Fritters

¾ cup of 1892 Traditional Ale beer
2 cups all purpose flour
2 eggs
2 lbs. melted butter
14 oz. tin clams, minced (save the clam juice)
½ cup saved clam juice
2 tsp. baking powder
Dash of salt

Combine all ingredients, except the clams.

Beat until smooth and add clams.

Deep fry at 350°F until golden brown. Place on a rack.

You can serve these with a curry or partridgeberry sauce.

Cocktails

Christmas Beer Nog

8 egg yolks
½ cup sugar
3 bottles of 1892 Traditional Ale beer
1 tsp. milk
Pinch of nutmeg

Beat the egg yolks and the sugar until smooth.

Gradually add the beer.

Beat until foamy.

Chill until cold.

McGuire's Cure

1 bottle of Honey Brown Light beer
½ cup sugar
3 cups raspberries
2 lemons

In a blender, reduce the raspberries and lemons to a juice.

Dip the edge of a wine or champagne glass in lemon juice to form a ring around the glass.

Put crushed ice in the glass.

Pour in the raspberry-lemon juice to cover half of the glass.

Fill with chilled beer and serve.

Pike's Smoothie

1 bottle Honey Brown beer
7 tbsp. sugar
3 tbsp. lemon juice
½ tsp. ground cinnamon

Mix together the lemon juice, cinnamon and sugar.

Add the beer and stir.

Chill and serve cold.

Quidi Vidi Cocktail

1 oz. fresh lemon juice
Pinch of ginger
Pinch of cinnamon
2 bottles of Honey Brown beer

Boil the beer, ginger and cinnamon for 3 to 5 minutes.

Pour in lemon juice and boil for one more minute.

Strain and chill.

Quick Quidi Vidi Cocktails

Dark Winter Night
Take 4 ounces of 1892 Traditional Ale and 4 ounces of Dark Rum, blend together and serve over cracked ice.

QV Float
Place a scoop of vanilla or chocolate ice cream in a large chilled beer glass and pour in a bottle of award-winning Eric's Red Ale, while taking care not to overflow the head of foam. Allow the head to settle before sipping the tasty delight.

Quidi Vidi Battery
Take 2 parts Iceberg Vodka, 2 parts Iceberg Rum, 3 parts Lemonade and 3 parts QV Lager for a robust tasting drink. Try it with 1892 Traditional Ale to add more flavours.

Shandy
Half a glass of QV Light and half a glass of gingerale served in a chilled glass.

Lambs Wool or Depth Charge
Start with a cup of apple sauce and 2 cups of 1892 Traditional Ale and combine in a sauce pan, then heat but do not boil. Stir in ¼ teaspoon of vanilla extract, ¼ teaspoon of powdered ginger and stir well. Sweeten with sugar or honey to taste and drink while hot.

Boilermaker
A shot of your favorite whisky and a mug of your favorite Quidi Vidi beer and you are ready for this experience.

Some like to shoot the whisky then use the beer as the chaser, otherwise, mix the two together to charge the beer.

QV Golden Lager and Lime
Add a dash of lime juice to a glass of QV Lager for a light refreshing taste on a summer's day.

Bite

Mix a Quidi Vidi Honey Brown half and half with cider to give a snappy drink.

Black Velvet Bind

Combine half a glass of Eric's Red Crème Ale with half a glass of Champagne to give a CO_2 fortified drink.

Beer Based Bloody Mary

Mix half a glass of QV Light with half a glass of tomato juice and add a dash of Tabasco and Worcestershire to get an amazing result.

Kissed in Quidi Vidi

This is a pleasant mixture of 1892 Traditional Ale beer and Cassis.

Grand Concourse

A mixture of Honey Brown beer and your favorite cola yields a light and refreshing beverage.

Red Eye

36 oz. tomato juice
1 bottle of Eric's Red beer
Dash of Worcestershire sauce and a dash of Tabasco sauce

Chill the beer and tomato juice and mix together.

Add the Worcestershire and Tabasco sauce.

Serve immediately.

Beer Trivia
In English pubs, ale is ordered by pints and quarts.
So in old England, when customers got unruly, the bartender
used to yell at them to mind their own pints and quarts
and settle down. Thus the phrase "mind your own P's and Q's".

Salads

Beer Coleslaw

4 oz. Honey Brown Light beer
8 oz. mayonnaise
1 oz. green pepper, finely diced
½ oz. onion, finely diced
1 medium sized head of green cabbage
2 tbsp. celery seed
Salt and pepper

Shred or finely slice cabbage with core removed.

Add green pepper, celery seed, onions, salt and pepper
to cabbage.

Mix mayonnaise and beer together and add to cabbage mixture.

Chef's Hint
You may add a little grated carrot.

Chicken and Beer Salad

2 lbs. skinless chicken breast
½ cup toasted almond slivers
16 oz. mesculine mix or baby spinach
2 mangos, peeled and medium diced
2 oz. QV Light beer
4 slices fresh ginger
4 cloves garlic
1 shallot, sliced
1¾ cups peanut oil
¼ cup sesame oil

Mix salad ingredients together and before service, add the dressing.

QV Shellfish Salad

8 oz. cooked lobster meat, chopped
4 oz. cooked scallops, whole
4 oz. cooked shrimp, whole
1 tsp. lemon juice
2 tbsp. QV beer
2 oz. green onion, finely diced
1 oz. celery, finely diced
1 oz. Dijon mustard
¼ cup yogurt
4 oz. mayonnaise
Salt and pepper to taste

Mix together the lobster, scallops, shrimp, green onion, celery.

Mix together the mustard, yogurt, mayonnaise, beer, lemon juice and salt and pepper. Add to seafood mixture.

Beer Potato Salad

3 lbs. potatoes, peeled
1 lb. celery, diced
1 medium onion, diced
4 oz. QV beer
8 oz. mayonnaise
3 tbsp. prepared mustard
2 tsp. salt
Dash of Tabasco sauce
Chopped parsley

Cook potatoes until tender (do not overcook). You can take them off the heat and strain when there is a little bone in them (al dente).

Dice.

Add diced celery and onion.

Mix together mayonnaise, mustard, beer, Tabasco sauce and salt.

Add potato mixture.

Blend all ingredients together.

Sprinkle with chopped parsley.

You can garnish with a tomato rose or sliced, hard boiled egg.

If colour is needed in salad, add grated carrot.

Caesar (Beer) Salad. Page 23.
Beer Potato Salad. Page 20.

Caesar (Beer) Salad

1 coddled* egg
2 large heads of romaine lettuce
½ cup olive oil
4 tbsp. QV Light beer
4 tbsp. lemon juice
1 cup croutons
2 cloves garlic
½ cup grated parmesan cheese
Salt and pepper

Rub bowl with garlic clove.

Tear lettuce in bite size pieces and put in bowl.

Mix olive oil, lemon juice and beer together and add to lettuce.

Toss lightly.

Add coddled egg, salt and pepper.

Toss.

Add croutons and cheese, and toss again.

Chef's Hints
You can add cooked turkey or chicken to make a meal.

*Coddle: Gently lowering the food into water that's come to a boil and removed from the heat.

Pasta Bows with Smoked Salmon

6 scallions, finely diced
4 tbsp. butter
6 tbsp. 1892 Traditional Ale beer
1¾ cup heavy cream
8 oz. smoked salmon
1 lb. bow tie pasta
Freshly squeezed lemon juice
2 tbsp. chopped fresh dill
Pinch of nutmeg

Melt the butter in a saucepan and add the scallions for 1 to 2 minutes.

Add the beer and boil to reduce to 2 tablespoons.

Stir in the cream and add nutmeg, salt and pepper.

Bring to a boil and simmer until thickened.

Cut the smoked salmon into squares and put in the sauce.

Add the cooked pasta and toss.

Serve immediately.

Note: Can be garnished with green peas.

Sauces & Soups

Barbeque Sauce

2 tbsp. butter
1 medium onion, finely diced
6 oz. celery, finely diced
2 oz. QV beer
2 oz. cold water
12 oz. tomato juice
3 tbsp. vinegar
¾ tsp. chili powder
1½ tsp. salt
¾ tsp. dry mustard
2 tbsp. brown sugar

Melt butter in a heavy sauté pan.

Add onion and celery and cook for 2 to 3 minutes.

Add dry ingredients and blend well.

Add liquids and simmer for 15 to 20 minutes.

Chef's Hint
Great for barbequing.

Chef Dinillo Salt Cod and QV Soup

1½ lb. boneless salt cod (soak for 24 hours in cold water
  and change water at least 3 times)
All purpose flour to dip salt cod
4 oz. olive oil
4 minced garlic cloves
1 medium red and green pepper, cut julienne
8 oz. diced potato
4 medium chopped onions
1 pinch crushed chili peppers
1 28 oz. tin Italian plum tomatoes, chopped
4 cups vegetable or fish stock
4 oz. QV beer
¼ cup fresh basil chopped or ½ tsp. dried
½ cup fresh parsley, chopped

Drain salt cod from water, pat dry and cut into cubes.

Dip in all purpose flour and fry in half the olive oil until tender.

Remove from pan and set aside.

In the same pan, add the remaining olive oil and sauté onion, garlic and red and green peppers until tender.

Add tomatoes, potatoes and stock.

Bring to a boil and simmer for 25 to 30 minutes.

Add beer, chili peppers, basil and salt cod and simmer for 5 minutes. Do not boil.

Taste for salt and pepper and adjust if needed.

Garnish with chopped parsley.

QV Light and Cod Ball Soup

½ lb. boneless cod fillet
½ lb. ground pork or bacon
1 oz. cornstarch mixed with 1 oz. cold water
1 bunch green onion, finely chopped
2 qt. chicken stock
1 oz. QV Light beer
6 tsp. rice vinegar
Salt and pepper to taste

Purée the cod and pork (or bacon) in a food processor and add the water and cornstarch. Blend well.

Shape mixture into balls.

Bring chicken stock to a boil and reduce to a simmer.

Cook (poach) the cod balls for 10 to 15 minutes in the simmering chicken stock. Do not boil.

Add the green onions, beer, rice vinegar and salt and pepper.

Garnish with chopped parsley.

Crab and QV Soup

¼ cup butter
1 oz. all purpose flour
1 oz. Worcestershire sauce
½ tsp. mace
4 hard boiled eggs
1 cup button mushrooms, finely chopped
2 lbs. cooked chopped crabmeat
1 cup minced celery
2 oz. scallions, minced
1 oz. butter
2 qt. scalded milk
2 cups scalded cream
4 oz. QV beer
Salt and pepper to taste

Mash the butter to a paste and add the flour, mace, eggs and Worcestershire sauce.

Mix the above with the crabmeat.

In a soup pot, sweat the mushrooms, celery and scallions in butter until cooked.

Stir in the scalded milk and cream.

Add the crab paste.

Add the beer.

Heat - Do not boil.

Adjust with salt and pepper and garnish with lemon zest.

Green Pea Soup with Mint and Tarragon

1 cup water
1 tsp. salt
2 cups fresh peas or one 10-oz frozen package
3 cups chicken stock or vegetable broth
1 tsp. chopped fresh mint or ½ tsp. diced
1 tsp. chopped fresh tarragon or 1 tsp. diced
4 oz Honey Brown Light beer
2 tbsp. softened butter
1½ tbsp. all purpose flour
1 cup whipping cream (heat)
2 tbsp. chopped fresh chives or 1 tsp. dried

Bring 1 cup water to boil in a saucepan and add salt.

Add the peas and cook until tender.

Drain the peas and transfer to a large mixing bowl.

Add the stock or broth, mint and tarragon.

Purée mixture in batches in a blender.

Transfer purée to a large sauce pan.

Add beer and cook over moderate heat for about 10 minutes, stirring occasionally.

Combine butter and flour in a cup, blend well and add to the hot soup and bring slowly to a boil.

Reduce heat and simmer until soup thickens 7 to 8 minutes.

Before serving, stir in heated cream and adjust seasoning.

Garnish with chopped chives and grated carrot.

Quidi Vidi Onion Soup

2 lbs. sliced onions (rings)
4 tbsp. butter
24 oz. QV beer
24 oz. chicken stock
24 oz. beef stock
2 tbsp. cornstarch
4 oz. light cream
1 tsp. sugar
Pepper

Sauté the onions in the butter until half done.

Add the stock, beer, sugar and pepper and bring to boil.

Simmer for approximately 30 minutes.

Mix the cornstarch and cream together until smooth.

Bring to a boil and add cornstarch and cream mixture.

Simmer for about 5 minutes.

Chef's Hints

*I did not include salt as most bases contain about 25%
and while the liquid will evaporate, the salt won't.*

*If a thinner soup is more desirable, don't add the
cornstarch and cream mixture.*

Croutons and cheese can be used.

Newfoundland Beer and Clam Chowder

2 lbs. fresh clams
1 bottle 1892 Traditional Ale beer
1 qt. water
6 oz. salt pork scrunchions
2 onions, finely diced
4 medium potatoes, medium diced
2 cups milk
1 cup light cream
Dash of Tabasco sauce
Salt and pepper to taste

Wash clams in cold water.

Place clams in a pot and cover with beer.

Bring to a boil and simmer until shells open.

Strain the liquid and save.

Remove clams from shells and discard shells.

Wash clams and chop roughly.

Sauté the pork scrunchions until half cooked and then add onions and cook until onions colour. Do not overcook.

Add clams and the saved liquid.

Add potatoes, Tabasco sauce and salt and pepper, and cook until potatoes are cooked.

Combine milk and cream together. Heat and add to chowder.

Chef's Hints
Chopped parsley is a good garnish.

Heat the milk and cream in a stainless steel pot. If heated in aluminum pot, it may have a grayish colour. Serve with a good crusty bread.

QV Light and Lamb Soup

2 onions, finely chopped
2 lbs. ground lamb
2 cups cooked rice
2 qt. beef stock
1 bottle QV Light beer
4 oz. minced parsley
Juice of 2 lemons
4 egg yolks
Dash of cayenne pepper
Salt and pepper to taste

Sauté onions in the butter until brown.

Put in a bowl and add lamb, rice, cayenne and salt and pepper.

Mix well and shape into 1 inch balls.

Roll balls in parsley.

Bring the stock and beer to a boil and reduce to 2 quarts.

Place the meatballs in a soup pot and pour the stock over them.

Simmer for 20 to 30 minutes.

Remove the meatballs.

Mix together the egg yolks and lemon juice.

Remove soup from heat and add the yolks and lemon juice.

Serve, garnished with parsley.

QV Light Scallop and Shrimp Chowder

2 qt. fish stock
4 oz. QV Light beer
2 cups onions, finely diced
½ cup all purpose flour
1 qt. half and half (cream and milk)
½ lb. scallops
½ lb. peeled and deveined shrimp
1 lb. frozen kernel corn
Bay leaf
½ cup butter
Salt and pepper to taste

Combine the fish stock, beer and bay leaf in a pot.

Bring to a boil and then simmer.

Remove and discard bay leaf.

In a soup pot, melt butter and add onions and sauté until half cooked.

Add the flour to make a roux and cook for a few minutes.

Heat the half and half and add to the roux stirring until it is thickened and smooth.

On a low heat, add the fish stock.

Add the corn and simmer until tender.

Add the scallops and shrimp and cook until done.

Adjust seasoning.

QV Light Consommé

28 oz. chicken stock
½ oz. dried mushrooms
1 tbsp. butter
1 small onion, diced
1 small carrot, diced
4 oz. button mushrooms, sliced
2 oz. wild rice
Pinch of salt, pepper and thyme
1 bay leaf
1 oz. QV Light

Soak dried mushrooms in half cup of the chicken stock until soft (about 15 to 20 minutes).

Drain, saving the stock.

Chop dried mushrooms.

In a soup pot, melt butter. Add onion and carrot and cook until tender.

Add remaining chicken stock, soaked and dried chopped mushrooms and reserved chicken stock, wild rice, sliced button mushrooms, thyme and bay leaf. Bring to a boil.

Simmer and cover for 30 to 40 minutes until rice is cooked.

Adjust seasoning and remove bay leaf.

Remove from heat and add beer.

Chef's Hint
*Remove bay leaf as it may lodge in windpipe
and make breathing very difficult.*

QV Light Soup

24 oz. mirepoix
8 oz. button mushrooms, medium diced
Roux; 6 oz. margarine or butter and 4-5 oz. all purpose
  flour
1 tsp. dry mustard
40 oz. chicken stock*
8 oz. sharp grated cheese
1 oz. grated parmesan or romano cheese
1 bottle QV Light beer
Salt and pepper

Note: If using base, be careful and read ingredients listed on
package as they may contain a high percentage of salt and MSG.

Melt margarine or butter in a soup pot and add the mirepoix and
sauté for 2 to 3 minutes. Do not brown.

Add flour and dry mustard and cook for approximately 2 minutes.

Keep stirring. **Note:** This will eliminate a starchy taste.

Add chicken stock and reduce heat to a simmer.

Add beer and cheeses to soup for 10 minutes.

Check seasonings.

To garnish, add some cooked, chopped spinach and blanched
red pepper to a bowl and ladle soup over.

Welsh Rarebit

2 lbs. sharp cheddar cheese, grated
15 oz. Eric's Red beer
½ tbsp. Worcestershire sauce
½ tbsp. dry mustard
½ tsp. paprika
Dash of Tabasco sauce
Dash of salt
6 slices of sandwich bread, toasted and trimmed

Place the beer in a large sauté pan or Dutch oven and bring to a boil.

Mix together the dry mustard, paprika, Tabasco sauce, Worcestershire sauce and salt, and stir until it's a smooth paste.

Add the beer.

Add the grated cheese, a little at a time, until all has been used.

Ladle the hot mixture over the toast. Serve at once.

May be garnished with Asparagus or Tomato or both.

Serves 6.

Moose Meatball and QV Soup

1 lb. ground lean moose meat
1 oz. butter
2 qt. beef stock
16 oz. QV beer
4 egg yolks
1 oz. lemon juice
16 oz. cooked rice
2 large onions, finely chopped
Chopped parsley to garnish
Dash of cayenne pepper
Salt and pepper to taste

Sauté the chopped onions in the melted butter until half cooked and add to the ground moose, cooked rice, cayenne pepper and salt and pepper.

Mix and shape into balls.

Combine the beef stock and beer and bring to a boil. Reduce to 2 quarts.

Put the moose meatballs in a soup pot.

Pour the hot stock and beer over them.

Bring to a simmer and cook for about 25 minutes.

Remove soup from heat.

Slowly mix the lemon juice to the beaten egg yolks.

Add to the soup.

Garnish with chopped parsley.

Fish & Seafood

Beer Battered Fried Fish

6 large pieces of cod fillet
  or haddock
Juice of 1 lemon
Salt and pepper
All purpose flour
Oil for frying

Batter
14 oz. all purpose flour
¾ oz. baking powder
¼ oz. sugar
¼ oz. salt
3 whole eggs
½ oz. salad oil
6 oz. 1892 Traditional Ale beer

Arrange the fish fillets in a dish and sprinkle them with lemon juice, salt and pepper.

Leave to stand for 30 minutes (in a refrigerator).

Place the all purpose flour, baking powder, sugar and salt in a bowl.

Place the eggs in a bowl and beat well.

Add the salad oil and beer and mix until thoroughly combined.

Add the dry ingredients and mix until a smooth batter is formed.

Let batter relax for about an hour.

Pat fish dry. Dust fish with flour and dip into batter.

Slowly slip fish into deep fryer at 350°F.

Cook until golden brown.

Chef's Hints

*Best to place on a cake rack when taking from deep fryer so excess fat will run off - serve with lemon, tartar sauce or coleslaw.
Put fish slowly into fat; if you drop it quickly it may stick to the basket.*

Beer Battered Fried Fish. Paqe 40.
Braised Halibut and Beer. Page 43.

Coquilles Quidi Vidi, Mornay. Page 47.
Blackened Halibut Fillet and Beer. Page 46.

Braised Halibut and Beer

1½ lbs. halibut fillets
12 oz. onion, medium diced
8 oz. button mushrooms
1 bottle 1892 Traditional Ale beer
2 cups diced tomatoes and liquid
Olive oil to coat pan
2 tbsp. Worcestershire sauce
2 tsp. chipalto hot sauce (Tabasco)
1 clover fresh garlic, finely chopped
Dash of chilli powder
2½ tsp. all purpose flour
Dash salt and pepper

Combine all dry ingredients in a bowl. Add halibut.

Heat oil in a deep sauté pan.

Add halibut and cook until lightly browned.

Take halibut out of the pan.

Add onions and mushrooms to same sauté pan until half cooked.

Add tomatoes and liquid, beer, and other liquids.

Bring to a boil and then reduce to simmer for 5 to 10 minutes.

Place halibut in sauce and simmer for approximately 2 to 3 minutes.

Serve with pasta.

Note: Don't leave halibut in sauce too long as it has a tendency to overcook and become dry.

Seal Flippers and Beer with Pastry

4 flippers (cleaned)
2 cups water
12 oz. Eric's Red beer
2 large onions, chopped
2 large turnips, large cut
4 jumbo carrots, large cut
2 parsnips, large cut
10 to 12 potatoes, large cut
Salt and pepper
½ tsp. savoury

Remove all fat from flippers.

Wash and pat dry with paper towel.

Put flippers in roast pan and braise at 450°F for about 10 minutes.

Turn flippers and add fat pork and braise at 450°F for about 15 minutes.

Add onions, water, savoury and beer and bake at 350°F until partly tender.

Add carrot, turnip, and parsnip and continue cooking.

When vegetables are half done, add potatoes.

When potatoes are done, add thickening and make a light gravy.

Chef's Hint
Do not parboil; soak in cold water with 2 teaspoons of baking soda for about 20 to 30 minutes. The baking soda makes the fat show white. All fat should be removed.

44

Topping

4 cups all purpose flour
4 tsp. baking powder
1 cup shortening
1 tsp. salt
Cold water - enough to make a stiff dough; add the water
  slowly.

Mix dry ingredients together and cut in shortening. When it is blended, add cold water until stiff but can roll.

Top flippers with pastry and vent it so some of the steam can escape during cooking.

Brush with egg wash.

Bake at 400°F for 20 to 25 minutes.

Beer Trivia

Before the invention of the thermometer, brewers used to check the temperature by dipping their thumb, to find whether appropriate for adding yeast. Too hot, the yeast would die. This is where we get the phrase " The Rule of the Thumb."

Blackened Halibut Fillet and Beer

(Serves 4 persons)

2 tsp. chili powder
2 tsp. Hungarian paprika
2 tsp. garlic powder, not garlic salt
2 tsp. all purpose flour
4 halibut fillet portions
Salt and pepper
8 tbsp. vegetable oil
2 oz. sun-dried tomatoes, chopped
1 oz. green onion, chopped
2 oz. button mushrooms, chopped
3 oz. 1892 Traditional Ale beer
8 oz. whipping cream

Mix all dry ingredients together.

Coat halibut.

Pan sauté on both sides in vegetable oil.

Finish cooking in a 350°F oven for 8 to 10 minutes.

In the same sauté pan, add sun-dried tomatoes, green onion and mushrooms with beer.

Add cream and reduce until thickened.

Ladle sauce on plate and serve halibut on top.

Garnish with parsley or lemon.

Chef's Hint
Make sure the pan and oil are hot when adding halibut as it will stick to a cold pan.

Coquilles Quidi Vidi, Mornay

2 oz. butter or margarine
10 oz. scallops
Lemon juice from 1 lemon
2 oz. QV beer
2 oz. sliced mushrooms
½ tsp. chopped shallots
8 oz. medium cream sauce
Salt and pepper to taste
2 oz. heavy cream/2 egg yolks - liaison
1 oz. grated cheese
Parsley, finely chopped

Sauté scallops in 1 oz. butter for 1 minute. Add lemon juice.

Remove scallops and place in shells or ramkins.

Sauté shallots and sliced mushrooms in remaining butter; add beer and liquor from scallops. Reduce to one third.

Add hot cream sauce.

Blend in liaison; season - Do not boil.

Pour sauce over scallops.

Sprinkle with cheese.

Brown in oven.

Sprinkle with parsley.

Honey Light Marinated Salmon

½ cup orange juice
½ cup Honey Light beer
2 oz. green onion, finely chopped
1 tbsp. Worcestershire sauce
1 tbsp. Dijon mustard
2 tbsp. orange zest
Salt and pepper
4 salmon fillets or steaks (6-7 oz portions)

Mix all ingredients together and pour over salmon and marinate for 3 to 4 hours in a refrigerator.

Grill for about 5 minutes on each side.

Great served with wild rice.

Beer Trivia
Long ago in England, pub frequenters had a whistle baked into the rim of their beer mugs or ceramic/glass cups. The whistle was used to order services. Thus we get the phrase, "wet your whistle."

Lobster and Beer Sauce

½ lb. lobster meat, cut in ½" squares
1 oz. margarine
¼ tsp. paprika
2 oz. 1892 Traditional Ale beer
16 oz. light cream sauce
¼ tsp. lemon juice
Salt and pepper

Melt margarine in a sauté pan and heat slowly.

Add paprika and lobster and sauté for 3 minutes.

Add beer.

Add lemon juice.

Add light cream sauce.

Season with salt and pepper.

Note: Serve with sauté fish.

Enjoy!

Beer Trivia
*To keep your beer glass or mug from sticking to your bar napkin,
sprinkle a little salt on the napkin before you set your glass down.*

Mussels, Tomatoes and Beer

2 lbs. mussels
1 bottle Eric's Red beer
2 tbsp. vegetable oil
2 oz. celery, medium diced
2 oz. onions, sliced
1½ oz. green pepper
1½ oz. red or yellow pepper
2 tsp. garlic, chopped fine
4 large tomatoes, medium diced
Salt and pepper

In a large sauté pan, sauté celery, onions, green pepper and garlic in oil for approximately 2 to 3 minutes over medium heat.

Add chopped tomatoes and cook for 5 to 7 minutes.

Add washed mussels and beer, and season with salt and pepper.

Stir and cover.

When mussels are done, (all shells are open) serve.

You may garnish with chopped parsley or chopped chives.

Serve with a good bread.

Mussels, Tomatoes and Beer Page 50

Pan Fried Halibut with Beer and Raisins. Page 53.

Pan Fried Halibut with Beer and Raisins

2 - 5 to 6 oz. halibut portions
2 oz. raisins
3 oz. QV beer
4 tbsp. clarified butter
Flour to dredge

Soak raisins in beer.

Heat butter in sauté pan.

Dredge halibut in flour.

Sauté until light brown on both sides.

Pour beer and raisins over halibut.

Bake in a preheated 375°F oven for 7 to 8 minutes.

Chef's Hints

A nice garnish for this would be fruit chutney. This includes; equal amounts of diced apple, pineapple and mango; dash of fresh grated ginger; and a red wine vinegar.

Combine all ingredients and cook until soft

Lobster, Beer and Salmon

Six 5-6 oz. salmon steaks
⅓ cup butter or margarine
1 small carrot, finely diced
1 small onion, finely diced
½ clove crushed garlic
1 cup QV beer
2 tbsp. tomato paste
¾ tsp. fennel seed
3 to 4 tomatoes, quartered
3 cups whipping cream
4 to 5 lobster shells

Sauté carrot, onion and garlic in butter or margarine for approximately 5 minutes.

Add lobster shells and fennel and cook for about 2 minutes.

Add beer, reduce to half.

Add remaining ingredients.

Simmer until thickened about 5 minutes.

Strain through a fine strainer.

Pan fry or poach salmon steaks.

Pour the sauce over the salmon steaks and garnish with chives, lemon zest, and parsley.

Chef's Hint

When pan frying fish, put fish in seasoned, all purpose flour and then egg wash (beaten egg and milk) and then add to a moderate heated frying pan that has oil in it. It will brown very quickly and may be finished in an oven, or refrigerate and cook it later. If the pan is cold, the fish will stick.

Mussels a la Reese

Normally we serve a pound of mussels per person
2 tbsp. vegetable oil
2 lbs. mussels
4 oz. red pepper, julienne
4 oz. celery, julienne
4 oz. onion, julienne
4 oz. polish sausage, sliced
2 oz. pineapple, medium diced (fresh or canned)
1 tsp. chopped garlic
3 oz. QV beer

In a suitable pot, add vegetable oil and when hot:

- Add garlic (do not brown) about 1 minute.

- Add red pepper, celery, onions and sauté for approximately 2 minutes.

- Add sausage and mussels; stir and cover.

- When mussels are opened, add the beer.

- Serve with a good bread and a Quidi Vidi brew.

Quidi Vidi Style Calamari

2 lbs. whole squid, fresh or frozen
2 tbsp. olive oil
2 cloves garlic, crushed
1 tsp. dill
6 oz. QV Light beer
1 tsp. lemon juice
Dash sugar
1 tbsp. flour
½ cup water
Salt and pepper to taste

Clean squid.

Cut mantles into 2 inch pieces.

Sauté garlic and squid in oil for 2 to 3 minutes.

Add dill and cook another 2 minutes.

Pour beer over mixture and cook for 20 minutes.

Add lemon juice and sugar.

Make a paste of water and flours, and add to squid mixture.

Cook until sauce thickens.

Season with salt and pepper.

Beer Trivia
Tossing salted peanuts in a glass of beer makes the peanuts dance.

Sandy Badger Shrimp

1 cup QV beer
1 lb. cold water shrimp, cooked
1 rib celery, diced
4 shallots, diced
1 onion, diced
3 tbsp. soft butter
1 tbsp. all purpose flour
Parsley
1 bay leaf
Salt and Pepper

Simmer the beer, celery, onion, shallots, bay leaf, and salt and pepper for 20 minutes.

Strain, saving vegetables and discarding bay leaf.

Mix the butter (melted) and flour together.

Bring liquid to a boil and add butter and flour, and cook until thickened.

Add shrimp and serve.

Beer Trivia
Monks brewing beer in the Middle Ages were
allowed to drink five quarts of beer a day.

Scallops and Quidi Vidi Light

2.2 lbs. High Liner individually quick frozen scallops, thawed
¼ cup butter or margarine
4 minced garlic cloves
2 tbsp. lemon juice
½ cup minced shallots
2 fresh tomatoes, seeded and finely diced
2 cups fish stock
2 cups QV Light beer
2 cups whipping cream
2 tbsp. chopped fresh thyme
¼ cup chopped fine fresh parsley
Salt and pepper to taste

Drain scallops; pat dry with paper towels.

In large frying pan, heat butter and add scallops, and cook for 2 to 3 minutes.

Add garlic and cook an additional 2 minutes, stirring frequently.

Stir in lemon juice.

Transfer scallops to a bowl; drain and reserve liquid from scallops. Set aside scallops and liquid.

In the same pan, add shallots; cook until softened.

Stir in tomatoes.

Deglaze pan with fish stock, beer and reserved liquid from scallops and reduce to about 2 cups.

Stir in cream and cook until sauce has reduced and thickened and measures about 3 cups.

Add thyme. Season with salt and pepper.

Return scallops to sauce; heat while stirring. Sprinkle with parsley.

Seafood with Beer Newburg

1 lb. lobster meat or crab meat, or peeled and deveined
  shrimp
1½ oz. butter
1 qt. medium cream sauce
Dash of lemon juice
2 oz. QV Light beer
½ tbsp. paprika
Salt and pepper

Place the butter in a saucepan and melt.

Add paprika and heat slowly.

Add the seafood that is being used.

Add the cream sauce and blend thoroughly with a wooden spoon.

Bring to a boil.

Add the beer and lemon juice.

Season with salt and pepper.

Remove from heat.

Chef's Hints
*You can use a chicken veloutè sauce with a
little cream instead of cream sauce.*

*To keep sauce from getting a skin on it, press
plastic wrap or waxed paper on it.*

Shrimp and Scallops in Beer

16 oz. raw, large shrimp, peeled and deveined
16 oz. raw scallops
3 tbsp. minced onion
4 tbsp. butter
2 tbsp. flour
8 oz. Honey Brown beer
½ tsp. thyme
1 tbsp. chopped parsley
2 tbsp. salt
Dash of Tabasco sauce
Juice of 1 lemon

Wash and dry scallops and shrimp.

Sauté shrimp, scallops and onion in butter for approximately 2 minutes.

Add salt, flour, and Tabasco sauce.

Add beer, lemon juice and thyme and bring to a boil, stirring constantly.

Reduce to a simmer and cook for another 5 minutes.

Sprinkle with parsley.

Serve with toothpicks.

Chef's Hint
*Cooking time may change depending
on the size of the shrimp and scallops.*

Meat & Game

Caribou and QV Light

½ cup butter
1 lb. butter mushrooms, sliced
4 white pearl onions, pealed
3½ lbs. boneless caribou, cut in 2" cubes
½ cup all purpose flour
2 cups beef stock
2 cups QV Light beer
4 oz. Screech
1 tbsp. tomato paste
4 cloves garlic, minced
1 tsp. dried thyme
1 bay leaf
Salt and pepper

In a heavy skillet or Dutch oven, melt half the butter.

Add mushrooms and brown very lightly; remove and set aside.

Add remaining butter to pan; add onions and brown; remove and set aside.

Add caribou, brown and remove from pan.

To fat in pan (there should be about ¼ cup; if not, add some) add flour, to make roux.

Add stock, beer, Screech and tomato paste and bring to a boil.

Add garlic, salt, thyme, bay leaf and pepper.

Put in casserole dish and bake at 350°F covered for approximately 2 hours.

Add onions and mushrooms.

Remove bay leaf. Adjust seasonings.

Beef and Beer Curry

1 clove garlic, minced
½ cup chopped onion
2 tbsp. vegetable oil
½ lb. ground beef (lean)
½ tsp. salt
1 tbsp. curry powder
2 tbsp. margarine or butter
2 tbsp. all purpose flour
¼ cup 2% milk
½ cup Honey Brown Light beer

Stirring frequently, sauté the onion and garlic in vegetable oil for about 5 minutes.

Remove and set aside the sautéed onions.

Brown the ground beef in the oil in the sauté pan.

Season with the salt.

Melt the butter in a saucepan; add the curry powder and then flour.

Cook for 2 to 3 minutes.

Add the milk mixed with the beer.

Bring to a boil but constantly stirring.

Add the onions and meat.

Note: Amount of curry powder may be increased to make it more spicy. This can be served in a small vol au vent as an appetizer.

Diced, cooked carrot, apple and raisins can be added to this dish to give it greater taste.

1892 Traditional Ale and Lamb Shank

4 lamb shanks
1 cup molasses
1 cup partridgeberries
1½ bottles 1892 Traditional Ale beer
1 cup chicken stock
Mirepoix: 1 cup of each, diced; carrot, celery, and onion

In a hot pan with vegetable oil, brown lamb shanks.

Add mirepoix and sauté until lightly brown.

Add beer and simmer for about 3 to 4 minutes.

Add molasses, berries and chicken stock to the pan.

Add the lamb shanks and mix thoroughly.

Put in a 350°F oven until lamb is tender (about 2 to 3 hours).

Beer Trivia

The Pilgrims landed at Plymouth Rock because of beer.
They had planned to sail further south to a warm climate,
but had run out of beer on the journey.

Eric's Red Chicken Lyonaisse

1 whole chicken, quartered
3½ lb. sliced potatoes
3 tbsp. butter
10 oz. diced ham or bacon
2 oz. chopped fresh herbs (rosemary, thyme and basil)
1 large sliced onion
2 carrots sliced on a bias
1 cup Eric's Red beer
Salt and pepper to taste

In a casserole dish, put down a layer of sliced potatoes. Put the chicken on top of this.

Add the ham or bacon, onions and carrots.

Season with the herbs, salt and pepper.

Pour beer over it.

Top with sliced potatoes.

Brush with melted butter.

Cover and bake at 350°F.

Remove cover for 20 minutes from the end of cooking to allow the potatoes to brown.

Quidi Vidi Brisket of Beef

Olive oil, enough to cover large sauté pan
4 to 5 lbs. beef brisket
Montreal steak rub marinade, prepared
2 cloves garlic medium diced
1 bottle of QV Light beer
½ tsp. chicken soup base
½ tsp. beef soup base
2 cups of mirepoit (chopped onion, celery, and carrot)

Place the oil in a deep sauté pan.

Season lightly both sides of the brisket with the rub marinade.

Add the meat and when it's seared on both sides, add the mirepoix, garlic, beer, and bases.

Add cold water and cover brisket and bring to a boil.

Put in a preheated 325°F oven and cook for 4 hours.

Remove from liquid and let rest for 20 to 30 minutes.

Cut across the grain thin.

Strain liquid and pour lightly over brisket.

Can be served with hot mustard or horseradish.

You can also serve baby red potatoes and root vegetables with the dish.

Beer Teriyaki

2 lbs. boneless sirloin, striploin or tenderloin
½ cup QV Light beer
¼ cup soya sauce
1 medium onion, cut brunoise
2 tbsp. sugar
1 clove garlic, minced
1 tsp. fresh ginger, minced

Cut meat into strips.

Combine all remaining ingredients.

Pour over strips and refrigerate for 4 to 5 hours.

Turn meat occasionally.

Broil for 2 to 3 minutes on each side.

Serve with broiled or grilled pineapple.

Beer Trivia
The oldest known written recipe is for beer.

Chicken Sauté and Eric's Red

Chicken breasts from 3 chickens
2 tsp. shallots, finely chopped
3 oz. Eric's Red beer
1 tbsp. paprika
1 cup supreme sauce
¾ pint heavy cream
2 oz. cooked ham, julienne

Sauté breasts in butter until golden brown and tender.

Remove breasts.

In same pan, cook shallot and beer, reduce to minimum.

Add paprika and supreme sauce.

Cook for about 3 to 5 minutes.

Strain sauce.

Add cream and ham.

Heat slowly and pour over chicken breasts.

Note: Supreme sauce is chicken stock thickened and added cream.

QV Light Velouté

24 oz. mirepoix
8 oz. button mushrooms, medium diced
Roux; 6 oz. margarine or butter and 4-5 oz. all purpose
  flour
1 tsp. dry mustard
40 oz. chicken stock*
8 oz. sharp grated cheese

1 oz. grated parmesan or romano cheese
1 bottle QV Light beer
Salt and pepper

Note: If using base, be careful and read ingredients listed on package as they may contain a high percentage of salt and MSG.

Melt margarine or butter in a soup pot and add the mirepoix and sauté for 2 to 3 minutes. Do not brown.

Add flour and dry mustard and cook for approximately 2 minutes.

Keep stirring. Note: This will eliminate a starchy taste.

Add chicken stock and reduce heat to a simmer.

Add beer and cheeses to soup for 10 minutes.

Check seasonings.

To garnish, add some cooked, chopped spinach and blanched red pepper to a bowl and ladle soup over.

Beer Trivia
Beer is the second most popular beverage in the world, coming in behind tea.

Caribou and Beer

2 lbs. caribou loin
4 oz. sour cream
4 oz. demi-glace
4 oz. Eric's Red beer
2 oz. paprika
2 oz. clarified butter
4 gherkins
1 lb. egg noodles or rice

Cut loin into strips and toss into seasoned paprika.

Heat skillet and add clarified butter.

Sea the strips of caribou - don't overcook.

Add beer and reduce.

Add demi-glace and reduce.

Cut the gherkins julienne and add to dish while cooking for about 10 minutes.

Serve with buttered noodles or rice.

Chef's Hint
Demi-glace means a rich brown stock reduced by simmering until it is only half of its original amount; a thick glaze that coats a spoon.

Chicken Cacciatore (1892)

5 whole chickens (between 2 & 2 ¼ pounds)
8 oz. all purpose flour
1 cup vegetable oil
12 oz. sliced mushrooms
9 oz. green peppers, cut into strips
12 oz. onions cut 1" long
½ tbsp. garlic minced
48 oz. crushed tin tomatoes and juice
4 oz. 1892 Traditional Ale beer
¼ tsp. oregano, crushed
Salt and pepper to taste

Clean and disjoint chicken. Remove rib bones from breast.

Dredge in seasoned flour.

Fry floured chicken in hot oil in a heavy skillet until lightly browned on both sides.

Place in roast pans.

Sauté mushrooms, green peppers, onions and garlic in a large saucepot in remainder of oil.

Cook about 10 minutes, add crushed tomatoes with juice, beer and seasoning.

Blend well, pour over chicken and bake at 350°F for 1 hour, or until done.

Great with pasta.

Chicken Breast Quidi Vidi with Crab and Shrimp

4 oz. crab meat, finely diced
4 oz. cold water shrimp, finely diced
2 oz. shallots, finely diced
2 oz. ricotta cheese
2 chicken breasts
2 tbsp. clarified butter
8 oz. 1892 Traditional Ale beer
8 oz. chicken velouté
2 oz. heavy cream
Salt and pepper

Place chicken on a cutting board, skin side down.

Using a boning knife, carefully make a pocket that runs the length of each breast.

Put stuffing in a pastry bag and poke the stuffing into each pocket.

Note: Do not overfill because the stuffing expands as it cooks.

Sauté the chicken in the clarified butter until well browned.

Transfer the chicken to a sheet pan and finish in a 350°F oven approximately 10 to 13 minutes.

De-glaze the sauté pan with the beer, simmer and reduce to half.

Add the velouté and cream

Adjust seasoning.

Ladle the sauce onto a warm plate and slice and fan the chicken breast on top.

QV Light Velouté

24 oz. mirepoix
8 oz. button mushrooms, medium diced
Roux; 6 oz. margarine or butter and 4-5 oz. all purpose
  flour
1 tsp. dry mustard
40 oz. chicken stock*
8 oz. sharp grated cheese
1 oz. grated parmesan or romano cheese
1 bottle QV Light beer
Salt and pepper

*Note: If using base, be careful and read ingredients listed on package as they may contain a high percentage of salt and MSG.

Melt margarine or butter in a soup pot and add the mirepoix and sauté for 2 to 3 minutes. Do not brown.

Add flour and dry mustard and cook for approximately 2 minutes.

Keep stirring. Note: This will eliminate a starchy taste.

Add chicken stock and reduce heat to a simmer.

Add beer and cheeses to soup for an additional 10 minutes.

Check seasonings.

To garnish, add some cooked, chopped spinach and blanched red pepper to a bowl and ladle soup over.

Chef's Hint
Use powdered fish stock for seasoning instead of salt and pepper.

Barbequed Steak and Beer

3 8-10 oz. steaks, tender cuts
8 oz. QV beer
2 tbsp. brown sugar
Dash of salt and pepper
Montreal steak spice marinade

Place steaks in shallow pan or sealed type bag and pour beer over them.

Marinate for approximately 1 hour, turning the steak over half way through.

Remove steaks and discard beer.

Combine other ingredients and rub over steaks and place in refrigerator for 15 minutes and then turn over. Rub the remaining side and let stand for 15 minutes.

Grill to the desired doneness.

Serve with a baked potato, sautéed mushrooms and onions, and a green salad.

Barbequed Steak and Beer. Page 74.
Moose and Brownie. Page 83

Moose Meatloaf and Mushroom and Beer Sauce. Page 86

Beer Moose Stroganoff. Page 77

Beer Moose Stroganoff

2 lbs. tender moose steak, cubed
2 oz. butter
12 oz. 1892 Traditional Ale beer
1 large onion
2 tbsp. all purpose flour
4 oz. sour cream
8 oz. sliced mushrooms (tin)
Dash of Worcestershire sauce
Salt and pepper

Brown the moose steak cubes on both sides in the butter.

Slice the onion and add.

Sauté moose and onions together for about 5 minutes.

Add the beer and Worcestershire sauce, salt and pepper.

Cover and simmer for approximately 2 hours or until the moose is tender.

Remove moose from pan.

Combine flour and water to make paste and add to gravy.

Add sour cream, mushrooms, salt and pepper.

Add moose to sauce.

Chef's Hint
Excellent served with pasta.

Chicken and Beer
(yield 6 servings)

3 - 2½ lb. chickens, disjointed
6 oz. fat bacon, cut into ½ inch pieces
1 clove garlic
12 oz. QV beer
12 oz. mushroom caps
8 oz. chicken stock
12 pearl onions, raw peeled
1 bay leaf
¼ tsp. thyme
6 oz. flour
Salt and pepper to taste

In a large sauté pan, place the fat bacon; cook until partially rendered.

Remove bacon and save.

Add the garlic cloves, cook slightly and remove them.

Flour each piece of chicken and fry in bacon fat until brown on both sides. You can also add vegetable oil if bacon fat is not sufficient.

Remove and keep warm.

Add the onions and mushrooms to the sauté pan; cook slightly.

Pour in the beer and chicken stock, bring to a boil and stir occasionally.

Place the chicken and bacon pieces in the pot.

Add thyme and bay leaf.

Cover and bring to a boil and then simmer.

Simmer for approximately 45 minutes or until tender.

Remove bay leaf.

Note: It's very important that bay leaves are removed before serving as it could lodge and block the air valve.

A good garnish for this dish is pearl onions and mushrooms.

Marinated Baby Back Ribs and Beer

5 lbs. baby back ribs, cut 2"x2"
2 bottles 1892 Traditional Ale beer
1 tsp. celery seed
3 tsp. light brown sugar
4 oz. honey
2 oz. chopped red, green or yellow pepper
1 tsp. liquid smoke
Dash of Worcestershire sauce

Mix all ingredients together and add baby back ribs.

Place in a sealed container and marinate overnight in a refrigerator.

Remove from marinade and BBQ over medium heat, turning every 3 to 4 minutes. When coming free from the bone, remove.

Serve with rice or vegetable stir fry.

Note: Can be brushed during cooking with marinade.

Eric's Red Kabobs

2 lbs. beef striploin or tenderloin
½ cup shallots, finely diced
1½ tsp turmeric or curry powder
1 bottle Eric's Red beer
5 tbsp. vegetable oil
1 tsp. fresh ground ginger
1 clove garlic, minced
Salt and pepper to taste
Large button mushrooms
Green peppers
Cherry tomatoes
Pineapple
Onions

Combine beer, oil, garlic, shallots, turmeric or curry powder, ginger and salt and peppers. Mix well.

Cut beef into 1½ to 2 inch cubes.

Pour marinade over beef.

Marinate for about 4 hours.

Drain meat, saving the marinade.

Using skewers that have been soaked in water for 30 minutes (if not, the skewers may burn), thread meat alternating with vegetables.

Broil kabobs about 4 inches from the heat source.

Brush the saved marinade over the kabobs.

Keep turning.

It takes about 15 minutes.

Flank Steak and 1892 Traditional Ale

8 boneless flank steaks
1 bottle 1892 Traditional Ale beer
2 rib of celery
3 cups onions, chopped
6 tbsp. vegetable oil
12 oz. beef stock (base or bouillion)
2 tbsp. cornstarch
4 tbsp. water
1 stalk parsley, chopped
Salt and pepper

Season the steaks with salt and pepper.

Sauté the steaks in the oil and brown lightly.

Remove steaks from pan.

Sauté onions in pan.

Put half the onions in a pan and arrange the steaks over them.

Put the remaining onions over the steaks.

Add the beef stock, beer and parsley to the flank steaks.

Cover and cook at 325°F for approximately 2½ hours.

Strain liquid and add the cornstarch to the water.

Bring liquid to a boil and add cornstarch mixture.

May 24th QV Light Hamburger

5 lbs. ground beef
1 cup onions, finely diced
20 oz. dry bread crumbs
7 oz. tomato juice .
6 oz. QV Light beer
Salt and pepper
Vegetable oil

Sauté onions in vegetable oil until half done.

Mix all remaining ingredients thoroughly.

Shape into 1 inch patties and chill.

Pan fry patties on top of stove for about 10 to 12 minutes.

Makes about 25 patties.

Chefs Hint
Make sure they are cooked to an internal temperature of 158°F.

Moose and a Beer

3 oz. Soya sauce or Oyster sauce
1 bottle 1892 Traditional Ale beer
4 minced cloves of garlic
Dash of salt and pepper
1 tbsp. cilantro, chopped
2 tbsp. parsley, chopped
3 (10 oz) moose steaks

Combine all ingredients.

Pour over steaks in a shallow pan and cover well or place in a sealed type bag.

Marinate for 6 to 8 hours.

Cook to desired doneness - BBQ.

Note: Tougher cuts will be marinated longer than tender cuts.

Serve with vegetable stir fry and rice pilaf.

Beer Trivia
Bavaria still defines beer as a staple food.

Moose and Beer Chili

6 tbsp. butter
3 lbs. ground moose meat
3 large onions, finely chopped
60 oz. crushed tomatoes (tin or fresh)
6 oz. tomato purée or paste
8 oz. QV beer
3 tbsp. chili powder
2 (28-oz.) cans red kidney beans
Dash of Tabasco sauce and pepper
1 tbsp. salt

Melt butter in saucepan.

Add onions and cook until tender.

Add moose and brown.

Add tomatoes, purée or paste, beer, salt, Tabasco sauce and chili powder.

Simmer for 15 minutes, stirring occasionally.

Add kidney beans and simmer for 10 to 15 minutes.

Serve with a good bread.

Serves 10 to 12 persons.

Moose and Brewis

3 cakes hard bread
1 tsp. salt
6 moose steaks (6 to 8 oz each)
1 large onion, chopped
18 oz. QV Light beer
18 oz. water
Thickening - a roux or whitewash
Lard

Soak hard bread overnight in plenty of cold water.

The next day, add salt and bring to a boil, strain at once. If not it will get soggy.

In a heavy skillet, add lard and seal both sides of the steak.

Add the onions and sauté for another 5 minutes.

Add water and beer, and cook to desired doneness.

Remove steaks from pan and thicken.

Place brewis on plate and top with moose and gravy.

Chef's Hint
This is excellent for camping as it isn't too heavy to carry in a knapsack

Moose Meatloaf and Mushroom and Beer Sauce

3½ lbs. lean ground moose
2 whole eggs
4 oz. milk
6 oz. bread, trimmed
2 oz. salad oil
4 oz. celery, finely diced
12 oz. onions, finely diced
Pinch of thyme, salt and pepper

Place bread in large mixing bowl and add milk and eggs.

Mix together and make a paste.

Add moose and sautéed onions, celery, and seasonings.

Put in loaf pans, lightly greased.

Bake at 350°F for approximately 1½ to 2 hours.

Remove from oven and lay on rack.

Don't cut immediately, let stand for 30 minutes.

To slice, turn the loaf over so the top crust becomes the bottom.

Place sauce on plate and arrange meatloaf on top and drizzle with more sauce.

Mushroom Beer Sauce

1 qt. brown sauce
4 oz. sliced mushrooms
4 oz. minced onions
¼ oz. minced garlic

8 oz. canned tomatoes and crushed
2 oz. butter
4 oz. Eric's Red beer
Salt and Pepper

Place butter in sauce pot and melt.

Add onions and garlic and sauté slightly.

Add mushrooms and sauté for about 1 minute.

Add the brown sauce and bring to a boil.

Add the tomatoes, salt and pepper and simmer for approximately 20 minutes.

Add beer.

Remove from heat.

If gravy is light in colour, add gravy browning.

Beer Trivia
*To get rid of the foam at the top of beer (the head),
stick your fingers in it.*

Moose Stew and QV Light

2 lb. moose, cut into cubes 1½" x 1½"
4 oz. all purpose flour
1 oz. margarine
1 oz. vegetable oil
48 oz. beef stock
2 medium onions, medium diced
3 large carrots, chopped roughly
1 medium turnip, chopped roughly
2 ribs of celery, medium diced
2 large tomatoes, medium diced
2 cloves of garlic, small dice
6 oz. QV light beer
Salt and pepper

Melt margarine and oil in a large pot and heat.

Mix the flour and moose together.

Add to pot with margarine and oil, and cook until its well browned. This will seal in the juices.

Add the beef stock and bring to a boil and reduce heat and simmer for approximately 1½ hours.

Add tomatoes and vegetables.

Add the beer and cook until vegetables are tender.

Add salt and pepper.

Chef's Hints

Be careful in using powdered bases as they contain high percentages of salt.

Marinated moose will give a better flavour.

Pork Sausages in Beer

12 Bratwurst sausages
1 tsp. butter
8 oz. 1892 Traditional Ale beer
2 tsp. cornstarch
Salt and pepper

Boil the sausages in water for approximately 5 minutes.

Melt the butter in a frying pan.

Brown the sausages.

Drain off the fat.

Add the beer and simmer for 15 minutes.

Add the cornstarch to a little of the beer to make a paste.

Season with salt and pepper.

Serve with mashed potatoes.

Chef's Hint
*The sausages can be cut into bite-sized portions
and served with toothpicks as an appetizer.*

Pork Tenderloin with Beer Sauce

1½ lbs. boneless pork tenderloin
5 oz. smoked bacon slices
2 shallots, chopped
8 oz. cream
4 oz. Honey Light beer
20 oz. sliced leeks
2 oz. butter
Salt and pepper

Preheat oven to 400°F.

Trim the fat from the tenderloin and wrap them in bacon, secure with toothpicks.

Heat a frying pan and brown on all sides.

Place in a baking dish and cook in the preheated oven for 15 minutes.

Remove the fillets.

Sauté the shallots in the fat from the baking dish.

Add the cream and reduce to half. Add the beer and simmer.

Remove the bacon from the fillets and save.

Sauté the leeks in the butter and season them with salt and pepper.

Slice tenderloin and serve on a bed of leeks, topped with chopped bacon and sauce.

Chef's Hint
Corn or apple fritters accompany this dish well.

Rabbit and Beer

1 cup vinegar
12 oz. QV beer
2 oz. flour
2 oz. fat back pork
2 large onions, chopped
1 tbsp. mixed pickling spices
1 tbsp. sugar
2 small rabbits; cut into serving portions
Salt and pepper to taste

Combine beer, vinegar, onions, pickling spices, salt and pepper in a large container.

Add rabbit.

Let marinate for 2 days in the refrigerator.

Turn the rabbit occasionally.

Remove rabbit from marinade and pat dry.

Dip rabbit in flour.

Render fat pork in a large skillet or sauté pan.

Add rabbit and brown. Drain off fat.

Strain marinade, add sugar and add to meat.

Bring liquid to a boil and then simmer.

Cover and simmer until rabbit is tender, about 30 to 40 minutes.

If desired, thicken liquid into a gravy.

Serve with a cold beer.

Note. A pinch of savoury may be used.

Roast Loin of Pork with Beer

2 lbs. pork loin
1 clove of garlic, crushed
8 oz. Honey Brown beer
1 oz. lard
8 oz. beef stock
2 onions quartered
Salt and pepper

Preheat oven to 425°F.

Cut a criss-cross pattern into the skin of the meat.

Mix the garlic, salt and pepper together and smear it over the surface of the pork loin.

In a heavy bottomed pan, brown the pork on all sides in the lard.

Place in a baking dish, cover with beef stock and roast for 45 minutes.

Add the onions.

Reduce the heat to 350°F and cook for 45 minutes more.

Serve hot with the cooking juices (beef stock).

Note: Stock may be thickened if desired.

Sauerbraten (Marinated in Beer)

4 lbs. boned shoulder of beef
3 tbsp. all purpose flour
3 oz. butter
1 lemon, sliced
Sugar to taste
Salt and pepper
4 oz. sour cream

Marinade
1 qt. QV beer
16 oz. water
1 lemon, quartered
2 bay leaves
1 onion, sliced
2 cloves
1 large tomato, peeled and chopped
6 peppercorns

Place the beef in a bowl.

Pour the marinade over the beef; refrigerate 2 to 3 days, turning the meat occasionally.

Remove the beef from the marinade.

Dry the meat (wipe), dust with the flour.

Brown it in butter in a saucepan.

Add 1 cup of strained marinade, lemon slices, sugar and salt.

Simmer, covered in a saucepan for approximately 3 hours or until tender.

Remove the beef, strain and purée the cooking liquid.

Add the sour cream and reheat the sauce - do not boil.

Pour the sauce served over the sliced meat.

Serves 8-10 persons.

Veal, Beer and Sour Cream

20 oz. veal cutlets
Flour to coat veal cutlets
8 oz. mushrooms
2 medium carrots
2 small onions
1 cup 1892 Traditional Ale beer
1 tsp. salt
1 tsp. pepper
Pinch of thyme
4 oz. sour cream

Sauté sliced carrots and onions until half cooked.

Cut veal cutlets into bite sized cubes.

Roll veal in flour.

Add to sautéed carrots and onions.

Cook for a few minutes to ensure veal is on both sides.

Add the 1892 Traditional Ale beer.

Add the sliced mushrooms.

Season with salt and pepper and thyme.

Cover and simmer for 20 to 30 minutes.

Before serving, stir in sour cream.

Serve with pasta.

May garnish with a dash of sour cream and chives.

Yankee Pot Roast in Beer a la Mode

4 lbs. rump roast, trimmed and tied
4 to 6 tbsp. vegetable oil
2 medium onions, chopped
4 stalks celery, chopped
2 cloves of garlic, chopped
1 qt. beef stock
2 bottles of Eric's Red beer
3 bay leaves
3 whole tomatoes, chopped

Heat oil in a large sauté pan and add rump roast.

Sear meat on all sides. This seals the juices in.

Add onions, celery, garlic, tomatoes, beer, bay leaves and beef stock.

Bring to a boil and reduce to simmer for approximately 2 to 2½ hours.

Remove roast from sauté pan and thicken liquid with a roux or whitewash.

Serve with vegetables (a la mode means served with); I serve julienne of carrot and turnip with the pot roast.

Slice pot roast after it cools - about 30 minutes.

Pour sauce over it, and garnish with vegetables.

Note: Tomatoes are a tenderizer and help in cooking.
Also, be careful in using bases as most contain MSG and a high percentage of salt. Can substitute moose for beef.

Eric's Chasseur

10 pieces chicken (legs, breast or thigh)
1 cup vegetable oil
4 oz. chipped onion
2 cloves garlic, finely chopped
1 lb. sliced button mushrooms
8 oz. Eric's Red beer
1 qt. fresh tomatoes, concasse*
1 cup tomato sauce
24 green olives
¼ cup fresh herbs, chopped

Season chicken with salt and pepper.

Brown chicken in oil in sauté pan.

To prepare sauce, remove all but half cup of the oil in pan.

Add chopped onions, garlic, mushrooms, beer and smother until tender.

Add tomatoes and smother a few more minutes.

Add tomato sauce.

Bring to a boil.

Pour over chicken.

Bake at 350°F until tender.

Add the olives.

Garnish with chopped fresh herbs.

---

*Concasse: Peeled, seeded and chopped.

Pasta

Baked Beans and Beer

2 cups navy beans
8 oz. salt pork, sliced with rind removed (bacon can be
  used as a substitute)
2 medium onions, chopped
2 bottles of Honey Light beer
4 oz. molasses
1 tbsp. prepared mustard
1 tsp. salt

Cover washed beans with cold water and soak overnight.

Drain and add fresh water to cover beans.

Bring to a boil, cover and cook over low heat for about
45 minutes.

Drain but save the liquid.

Mix together the molasses, mustard, beer and salt.

Pour over the drained beans mixed with the salt pork.

Add enough of the saved liquid to cover the beans.

Bake at 275°F for approximately 6 hours, stirring occasionally.

Add the bean liquid if needed.

Serve with sausages and a good bread.

Clams-1892 Traditional Ale and Pasta

12 clams, live
4 oz. water
3 oz. 1892 Traditional Ale beer
3 tbsp. olive oil
3 tbsp. chopped parsley
1 chopped garlic clove
½ lb. cooked spaghetti, linguine or fettuccini
Salt and pepper to taste

Wash the clams well in cold water.

Put the clams in a large saucepan with the water and beer.

Cover and steam until the shells open, about 8 to 10 minutes.

Remove the clams from the shells and chop.

Strain the cooking liquid (beer and water mixture).

Put the strained liquid in a saucepan. Boil and reduce to half.

Heat the oil in a large sauté pan, add the garlic and cook for about 3 to 4 minutes (do not brown garlic).

Add the reduced liquid. Add the cooked pasta.

Add the chopped clams.

Cook for about 5 minutes on a medium heat.

Season with salt and pepper. Garnish with chopped parsley.

Chef's Hint

Any shells that are not opened, discard

Mussels QV Light and Pasta

5 lbs. mussels
1 cup heavy cream
3 chopped shallots
1 cup QV Light beer
1 chopped garlic clove
3 tbsp. butter
1 pinch of saffron
12 oz. pasta bows (any pasta will do)
Salt and pepper to taste
Garnish with chopped parsley

Wash the mussels well under cold water.

Cover the mussels with the beer and shallots in a large pot.

Cover and cook over a high heat for about 8 minutes until the shells have opened.

Strain the liquid from the mussels and save.

Shell all the mussels.

Bring the saved liquid to a boil. Reduce by half.

In a large sauté pan, melt the butter and add the chopped garlic and flash (cook) for about 2 minutes.

Pour in the mussel liquid, cream and saffron.

Heat until sauce thickens. Add mussels.

Add pasta and garnish with chopped parsley.

Chef's Hint
This can be garnished with mussels in the shell.
Any mussels that aren't opened, discard.

Moose and Spaghetti Sauce

1 clove of garlic, crushed
3 lbs. ground moose meat
16 oz. onion, chopped fine
16 oz. green pepper, chopped fine
12 oz. celery, chopped fine
16 oz. Eric's Red beer
2 tins tomato paste
2 tins tomato sauce
2 (28 oz.) crushed tomatoes
1 bay leaf
¼ tsp. thyme
¼ tsp. rosemary
2 tbsp. brown sugar
Dash of hot sauce
Dash of cayenne pepper
Salt and pepper
2 tbsp. vegetable oil

Fry ground moose and set aside.

In a heavy bottomed saucepot, sauté onion, garlic, green pepper, and celery for 3 to 5 minutes.

Add remaining ingredients and bring to a simmer.

Add ground moose and simmer for 1½ to 2 hours.

Season to taste.

Before serving, remove and discard bay leaf.

Serve with pasta, cheese and a good bread.

Chef's Hint
Bay leaf, if not removed, could lodge in someone's windpipe and make breathing very difficult.

Pasta with Shrimp and Peas

3 tbsp. olive oil
2 tbsp. butter
2 scallions, chopped
3 cups ice water shrimp
1 cup frozen green peas, thawed
14 oz. bow tie pasta
8 oz. QV Light beer
Pinch of saffron
Salt and pepper
Garnish with fresh dill

Heat the oil and butter in a frying pan.

Sauté the scallions lightly.

Add the shrimp and peas, and cook for 2 to 3 minutes.

Stir in beer and saffron into the shrimp mixture.

Increase the heat and reduce the liquid to about half.

Add salt and pepper.

Add the cooked pasta to the sauce.

Garnish with fresh dill.

Pasta QV and Sun-Dried Tomatoes

1 rib celery, finely diced
1 cup sun-dried tomatoes, finely chopped
1 lb. fettuccini
10 whole tomatoes
½ cup QV beer
1 crushed garlic clove
Salt and pepper to taste

Put the celery, garlic, sun-dried tomatoes and beer in a large saucepan.

Cook for about 10 to 15 minutes on a medium heat.

Put the tomatoes in boiling water for about 2 to 3 minutes.

Remove and place in cold water.

Peel, cut and remove the seeds (concasse).

Chop the tomatoes and add to the saucepan.

Simmer for about 5 to 7 minutes.

Add cooked pasta to the sauce and serve immediately.

Great served with breaded fried chicken or pork cutlet.

Pasta and Beer and Cold Water Shrimp

Vegetable oil to cover bottom of sauté pan
1 bottle of Eric's Red beer
20 oz. cold water shrimp, cooked
Dash salt and pepper
8 oz. thinly sliced onion rings
4 oz. blanched diced red, green or yellow pepper
2 garlic cloves, minced
Dash lemon or lime juice
32 oz. cooked pasta
* spaghettini, vermicelli
* fettucine or linguine
cook al dente (to the tooth)

In a large sauté pan or Dutch oven, add vegetable oil; and when hot, add onion rings, blanched pepper and garlic.

Sauté about 2 to 3 minutes and add beer.

Bring to a boil; cook 2 to 3 minutes at a simmer.

Add shrimp, lemon or lime juice, and stir occasionally.

Add pasta and toss.

Serve with chopped chives or a dash of parmesan cheese.

Enjoy!

Serves 4 to 6 persons.

Vegetables

Barbequed Onions in Beer

White or red onions, medium size
QV beer
Butter
Garlic salt
Black pepper
Aluminum foil

Peel and wash onions.

Place in beer and marinate for 30 to 45 minutes.

Cut a cross in the top of each onion.

Place a large piece of butter in the cross.

Sprinkle with garlic salt and pepper.

Wrap in aluminum foil.

Place on BBQ and cook until tender, about 12 minutes.

Chef's Hint
For BBQ's, use a heavy aluminum foil.

Barbequed Onions in Beer. Page 106.
Scalloped Potatoes and Beer. Page 100.

Scalloped Potatoes and Beer

2 lbs. sliced potatoes
2 large sliced onions
1 cup QV beer
1 cup chicken stock
¼ cup butter
½ cup bread crumbs
¼ cup grated cheese
Dash of garlic powder (not garlic salt)
Dash of salt and pepper

Layer potatoes and onions in a baking dish.

Add chicken stock and beer.

Season.

Cover and bake at 350°F for 30 to 40 minutes.

Melt butter and add bread crumbs, cheese and garlic powder.

Uncover and put crumb mixture on top and bake at 325°F until potatoes are tender.

Chef's Hint

You can partially cook potatoes before to save time.
Put sliced potatoes in salted water and cook al dente (a little hard).

Beer Batter Onion Rings

10 oz. all purpose flour
2 tsp. baking powder
1 egg
16 oz. 1892 Traditional Ale beer
Onions
Salt and Pepper

Sift dry ingredients together.

Beat the egg in a separate bowl. Add the beer to the beaten egg.

Add the egg and beer mixture to the dry ingredients, mix season with salt and pepper.

Peel and cut onions into rings.

Dust with flour.

Dip in batter and deep fry at 350°F until golden brown.

Remove from fryer and place on a cake rack.

Beer Trivia
Beer is a source of B- complex vitamins.

Beer Velouté Sauce

4 oz. butter or margarine
4 oz. all purpose flour
1 qt. chicken stock
4 oz. QV beer
Salt and pepper

Heat butter or margarine in sauce pan.

Add flour.

Add hot stock and beer slowly, whipping constantly until thick and smooth.

Adjust seasoning.

Ladle sauce on plate and arrange vegetable strudel on top.

Makes 1 quart.

Beer Trivia
In Japan, beer is sold in vending machines, by street vendors and in the train stations.

Herbed QV Potatoes

2 lbs. baby red potatoes, cut in half
2 crushed garlic cloves
4 tbsp. olive oil
2 oz. beef stock
2 oz. QV beer
2 tsp. chopped rosemary
3 tsp. chopped thyme
1 pinch dry mustard
1 pinch turmeric
Salt and pepper to taste

Wash, pat dry and place the baby red potatoes in a large bowl.

Mix all the remaining ingredients together and add to potatoes.

Put in roasting pan.

Cover and bake at 350°F until half done.

Remove cover and finish cooking.

Chef's Hint
Large potatoes can be used; cut them into large wedges.

Beer and Sweet Corn

36 oz. Honey Light beer
6 husked fresh corns on the cob
Salt
Butter, melted

Simmer beer.

Add corn.

Bring to a boil.

Cook for 5 minutes.

Remove and add salt and melted butter.

Vegetable Beer Dip

3 oz. cream cheese
4 oz. cottage cheese
1 oz. green onion, finely diced
1 tsp. capers
1 tsp. grated parmesan cheese
1 tsp. prepared mustard
1 tsp. paprika
3 oz. QV Light beer

Blend all ingredients together and chill until ready to serve.

Great with celery, carrots or broccoli.

Squash in Beer

Olive oil
1½ lbs. peeled and diced zucchini, eggplant or any
  desirable squash
8 oz. chopped prosciutto (Italian ham)
10 oz. Honey Brown beer
½ tsp fresh rosemary, chopped
½ tsp fresh tarragon, chopped
4 oz. chopped blanched red pepper
4 oz. chopped blanched green pepper
1 lb. cooked pasta, penne or rotini
Salt and pepper
Parmesan cheese

In a large deep sauté pan, add oil.

Add squash.

Cook for about 15 minutes.

Add prosciutto, beer, rosemary, tarragon, salt and pepper.

Reduce the liquid by half.

Add chopped blanched peppers.

Add the cooked pasta.

Add the meat and garnish with cheese.

Desserts

Beer Tea Biscuits

⅔ cup Honey Light beer
⅓ cup grated parmesan cheese
2 cups all purpose flour
3 tbsp. butter
½ tsp. salt
5 tsp. baking powder

Mix together all the dry ingredients.

Cut in butter until its crumbly.

Add beer to make a dough (soft).

Knead dough on floured board.

Roll ½ to ¾ inch thick and cut with a floured cutter.

Bake on ungreased cookie sheet pan at 425°F for approximately 10 to 15 minutes.

Beer Crêpes

2 eggs
8 oz. QV beer at room temperature
8 oz. all purpose flour
½ tsp. salt
Melted unsalted butter or vegetable oil for pan

Break eggs in a bowl and beat with a whisk.

Add beer and flour.

Beat until smooth.

Add salt and let batter relax 30 to 45 minutes.

Heat a 7" crêpe pan.

Brush lightly with melted butter or oil.

Add 4 tablespoons of batter and very quickly tilt and rotate the pan until the bottom is covered.

Cook until lightly brown on one side and then turn it over and cook the other side.

Slide off pan on waxed or parchment paper.

Note: Make sure pan is greased for each crêpe.

Beer Fingers

¾ cup all purpose flour
¾ cup rolled oats
¼ cup soft butter or margarine
½ cup Erics Red beer
¼ tsp. ground cinnamon
¼ tsp. salt
1 tsp. ginger

Mix all dry ingredients together.

Add softened butter and crumble with fingers.

Add beer and mix enough to blend.

Put in a well greased 9" sheet pan.

Spread evenly.

Bake at 425°F for 20 minutes.

Cool and cut in fingers.

Beer Crepes. Page 117.
Beer Fingers. Page 118.

Beer Spice Cake. Page 121.
Beer Tea Biscuits. Page 116.

Beer Spice Cake

2 cups all purpose flour
1 tbsp. baking powder
¼ tsp. salt
¾ cup butter
1½ cups brown sugar
8 oz. Honey Light beer
3 eggs
2 tsp. cinnamon
1 tsp. nutmeg
1 tsp. ginger

Mix all dry ingredients together.

Cream the butter and add the sugar slowly.

Separate eggs.

Beat egg yolks and add slowly to the creamed mixture.

Add the dry ingredients slowly with the beer.

Beat egg whites until stiff and fold in.

Pour into greased or line cake pans.

Bake at 350°F for about 25 to 30 minutes.

Date and Nut Beer Cake

2 cups brown sugar
1 cup butter
2 eggs
1 cup chopped nuts
2 cups chopped dates
1 tsp. cinnamon
½ tsp. allspice
½ tsp. ground cloves
2 cups QV Light beer
3 cups all purpose flour
2 tsp. baking soda
½ tsp. salt

Cream butter and sugar.

Stir in eggs, nuts, dates and spices.

In a separate bowl, mix together flour, baking soda and salt. Stir in beer.

Combine beer mixture with creamed mixture and mix until well blended.

Bake in a large tube pan in a 350°F oven for approximately 1 hour and 15 minutes, or until cake tester comes out clean.

Raisin Beer Cake

1¾ cups all purpose flour
¼ cup butter or margarine
1 cup molasses
1 cup seedless raisins
½ tsp. salt
1½ cups 1892 Traditional Ale beer
1 tsp. baking powder
¼ tsp. baking soda
1 cup chopped walnuts
1 tsp. cinnamon
1 tsp. nutmeg
¼ tsp. ginger

Mix together flour, salt, baking powder, baking soda, cinnamon, nutmeg, and ginger.

Combine the butter, molasses, and beer in a sauce pan. Stir in the raisins and heat until butter melts.

Cool for 20 minutes.

Add the dry ingredients to the beer mixture and stir until smooth.

Add the nuts.

Bake in a 9" greased, flour-dusted tube pan in a preheated oven at 350°F for one hour.

Turn out on a rack to cool.

Fruit Beer Cup

1 cup hulled strawberries
2 peeled and stoned peaches
2 slices pineapple
2 oranges, peeled & cut into segments
2 bottles Honey Light beer
1 tbsp. sugar

Cut the fruit into small pieces and marinate them in the beer for 12 to 14 hours.

Before serving, taste.

Add sugar.

Place the fruit and the beer in which it was marinated into 4 glasses and top with fresh beer.

Beer Trivia

The first consumer protection law ever written was enacted over beer by Duke Wilhelm IV of Bavaria in 1516. It was a purity law limiting the ingredients of beer to barley, hops and water.

Date and Nut Beer Cake. Page 122.
Fruit Beer Cup. Page 124.

Grandmother's Gingerbread. Page 128.
Hush Puppies. Page 127.

Hush Puppies

4 oz. QV Light beer
12 oz. milk
16 oz. (2 cups) corn meal
1 egg
2 oz. grated onion
2 tsp. baking powder
1 cup flour
Dash of salt

Mix the dry ingredients together.

Add onion and mix.

Beat egg.

Add beaten egg to milk and beer.

Add to dry mixture.

Shape.

Deep fry at 350°F until golden brown.

Note: Their name (hush puppy) is said to have come from the fact that, to keep hungry dogs from begging for food while the dinner was being prepared, cooks used to toss scraps of the fried batter to the dogs with the admonition "Hush Puppy."

Grandmother's Gingerbread

1 medium egg
⅓ cup brown sugar
⅓ cup molasses
⅓ cup butter
1 tsp. baking soda
¼ tsp. baking powder
½ tsp. salt
1 tsp. cinnamon
1 tsp. ginger
1¾ cup flour
4 oz. 1892 Traditional Ale beer

Beat egg.

Combine with brown sugar, molasses and melted butter.

Mix dry ingredients together.

Add to first mixture alternately with beer.

Pat into greased 8" square pan and bake at 350°F for approximately 30 to 35 minutes.

Chef's Hint
You can add raisins if desired.
Great served with custard and whipped cream.

Patty's Beer Cake

2 cups brown sugar
1 cup shortening
2 medium eggs
2 cups chopped dates
1 cup chopped walnuts
3 cups all purpose flour
2 cups 1892 Traditional Ale beer
2 tsp. baking soda
½ tsp. ground cloves
½ tsp. allspice
1 tsp. cinnamon
½ tsp. salt

Cream shortening and sugar.

Stir in eggs, walnuts, dates and spices.

In a separate bowl, combine flour, baking soda and salt.

Stir in beer.

Combine beer mixture with creamed mixture and mix until well blended.

Grease pan with shortening or oil and dust with flour, removing excess flour.

Bake at 350°F for approximately 1 hour and 15 minutes.

Test cake with toothpick, if it comes out clean when inserted in the cake, it is baked.

Nellie's Boiled Pudding

1 cup chopped walnuts
¼ cup diced citron
2 cup raisins
½ cup suet*, minced or
  ground
2 small granny smith
  apples, peeled and
  medium diced
½ cup all purpose flour
¼ cup sugar

¾ cup bread crumbs
½ cup molasses
½ cup QV Light beer
2 eggs, beat slightly
1 tsp. baking powder
½ tsp. baking soda
½ tsp. cinnamon
½ tsp. salt
¼ tsp. ground cloves
¼ tsp. allspice

In a bowl, put apple, citron and raisins.

Pour beer over the above and let stand for about an hour and a half.

Add beaten eggs and molasses.

Add bread crumbs, walnuts and suet.

Stir in remaining ingredients.

Put pudding mixture in a greased 2 quart mold with a tightly fit cover.

If you don't have a cover, cover top with plastic wrap and cover with aluminum foil and tie tightly with string.

Place on a cake rack in a pot and pour in boiling water to ½ to ¾ depth of the pudding mold.

Steam for approximately 5 to 6 hours.

Add more water as it reduces.

Suet: *Found in beef, sheep and other animals, suet is the solid white fat found around the kidneys and loins. Many recipes call for it to lend richness to pastries, puddings, stuffings and mince meats.*

Can be served with:

Hard sauce
½ cup butter
½ tsp. vanilla extract
1¼ cup confectioners sugar
⅓ whipped cream

Cream butter. Slowly add sugar and vanilla. Fold in whipped cream.

Molasses Sauce
1 cup molasses
1 tbsp. butter
Dash of nutmeg

Boil together for about 3 minutes

Partridgeberry Sauce
1 cup partridgeberries
¾ cup sugar
¾ cup boiling water

Boil together until the berries are soft. The sauce will thicken (about 15 to 20 minutes).

Lemon Sauce
1 cup granulated sugar
3 tbsp. all purpose flour
2 tbsp. butter
2 cup boiling water
Grated rind and juice of 1 lemon
Dash of salt

Mix flour, sugar and salt together. Gradually add the boiling water. Stir to keep the mixture smooth. Take from heat and add lemon juice and rind. Serve hot.

Pears and QV Light

4 bartlett pears
⅔ cup QV Light beer
⅔ cup orange juice
2 cups brown sugar
2 crushed juniper berries

Core the pears and leave whole.

Mix all the remaining ingredients together.

Bring to a boil.

Add the pears and simmer for about 20-25 minutes.

Baste occasionally.

Chef's Hint
Do not cover as pears will overcook.

TEMPERATURE EQUIVALENTS

	Fahrenheit	Celsius
Freezer	0°	-18°
Water Freezes	32°	0°
Refrigerator	40°	4°
Wine Storage	55°	13°
Room Temperature	68°	20°
Lukewarm	98.5°	37°
Simmering	180°	82°
Water Boils	212°	100°

APPROXIMATE METRIC EQUIVALENTS

¼ teaspoon . . . . 1 ml
½ teaspoon . . . . 2.5 ml
¾ teaspoon . . . . 4 ml
1 teaspoon . . . . 5 ml
1 tablespoon . . . . 15 ml
2 tablespoons . . . . 30 ml
½ cup . . . . 118 ml
1 cup . . . . 237 ml
2 cups (1 pint) . . . . 473 ml
4 cups (1 quart) . . . . .95 litres
4 quarts (1 gallon) . . . . 3.8 litres
1 gram . . . . .035 ounce
7 grams . . . . ¼ ounce
28 grams . . . . 1 ounce
113 grams . . . . 4 ounces
227 grams . . . . 8 ounces
454 grams . . . . 16 ounces (1lb)
1 kilogram . . . . 2.2 lbs

ABBREVIATIONS

Ounces .... oz.
Teaspoon .... Tsp.
Tablespoon .... Tbsp.
Pounds .... Lbs.
Quart .... Qt.

MEASUREMENT EQUIVALENTS

Pinch/Dash .... ⅟₁₆ teaspoon

½ teaspoon .... 30 drops

1 teaspoon .... ⅓ tablespoon

3 teaspoons .... 1 tablespoon

½ tablespoon .... 1½ teaspoon

1 tablespoon .... 3 teaspoons; ½ fluid ounce

2 tablespoons .... 1/8 cup; 1 fluid ounce

3 tablespoons .... 1½ fluid ounces

4 tablespoons .... ¼ cup; 2 fluid ounces

8 tablespoons .... ½ cup; 4 fluid ounces

12 tablespoons .... ¾ cup; 6 fluid ounces

16 tablespoons .... 1 cup; 8 fluid ounces; ½ pint

2 cups .... 1 pint; 16 fluid ounces

4 cups .... 1 quart; 32 fluid ounces

1 pint .... 2 cups; 16 fluid ounces

1 quart .... 2 pints; 4 cups; 32 fluid ounces

4 quarts .... 1 gallon; 8 pints; 128 fluid ounces

8 quarts .... 1 peck

4 pecks .... 1 bushel

RECOMMENDED SAFE COOKING TEMPERATURES

	Fahrenheit	Celsius
Beef/Lamb		
Rare	140°	60°
Medium	160°	71°
Well Done	170°	77°
Ground Meats		
Beef/Pork/Lamb	160°	71°
Pork		
Roast/Chops	160° to 165°	71° to 74°
Rabbit	180°	82°
Stuffing - Poultry	180°	82°
Turkey		
Bone in	180°	82°
Boneless	170°	77°
Chicken/Ducks	175° to 180°	79° to 82°

HOW TO CLEAN A SQUID
Procedure No. 1 – For strips, pieces, etc.

Thaw frozen squid.

From opening in mantle of squid, cut mantle with knife lengthwise.

Take out chitinous pen. With knife, scrape away any visceral remains adhering to the inside of the mantle wall. Turn mantle to other side.

Spread inside of mantle open flat. Pressing mantle with one hand, grasp head and arms and pull off intestines at same time.

Starting with tail end, pinch fins, pulling fins and outer membrane from mantle. Remove any remaining membrane with knife. Wash squid under cold running water. Cut mantle into desired strips. In recipes that require cutting into strips, pieces, etc., be sure to check if cutting should be done before or after cooking.

Procedure No. 2 – For stuffing and rings

Thaw frozen squid. Hold mantle with one hand. With other hand, grasp head and arms, and pinch quill at opening to separate from mantle. While holding on the chitinous pen and head, remove pen, head, and intestines with pulling motion. Starting with tail end, pinch fins, pulling fins and outer membrane from mantle. Peel off remaining membrane. Turn mantle inside out by pushing smaller end through large opening. With knife, scrape away any remaining viscera. Wash thoroughly. Stuff or make into rings by cutting across mantle. Be sure to check if cutting should be done before or after cooking.

Tentacles and Arms: Squid has two tentacles and eight arms. Cut across head in front of eyes to retain arms. Squeeze out round sack containing beak. Skin may be removed from arms by placing arms in boiling water for 2-3 minutes. Take off skin by tightening fingers around the arms and pulling skin.

Note: Cooking Squid: In recipes for cooking squid in boiling, salted water, bring enough water to boil to cover amount of squid to be cooked. Add salt to taste. Add squid.

SAFETY RULES

1. Use dry towels or oven mitts when handling hot pans.

2. Remove the lids of pots slowly, lift the side away from you.

3. Avoid over-filling hot food containers.

4. Never let the long handles of pots and pans extend to the front of the stove.

5. Have a fire extinguisher.

6. Never have glass near any food, it may break or chip.

7. Do not grab for falling knives.

8. Knives should never be placed in drawers. They should always be placed in a knife rack for proper storage.

9. Always use a sharp knife – it is safer than a dull one.

10. Pick up knives by the handle only.

11. When slicing round objects such as onions or carrots, cut a flat base so the object will set firmly and will not shift when being cut.

12. When using electrical power equipment, always follow manufacturer's instructions and recommendations.

13. When pan frying food always turn food away from you.

14 If using a kitchen meat grinder (attachment for mixer), use a stomper.

15. If anything is spilled on the floor, clean it up immediately.

16. Do not throw water on a grease or fat fire.

SANITATION RULES

1. Keep foods covered as much as possible; use clean utensils.

2. Purchase inspected meat.

3. Exercise caution when using leftovers.

4. Cook all pork thoroughly.

5. Make sure bent cans have not been punctured.

6. Do not expose food to the danger of temperatures 40°F to 140°F for more than a 3 hour period.

7. Check all fish and shellfish for freshness.

8. Do not refreeze thawed meat, fish or vegetables.

9. Wash all fruits and vegetables.

10. Purchase pasteurized milk.

11. If ever in doubt, THROW IT OUT.

12. Avoid cross-contamination.

GLOSSARY

ALE
A category of alcoholic beverages brewed from a combination of hops and barley malt, where the yeast rises to the top of the fermentation tank. Ale is typically stronger than beer.

BEER
A generic term for low-alcohol beverages brewed from a mash of malted barley and other cereals (like corn, rye or wheat) flavoured with hops and fermented with yeast. Technically, beers are only those beverages in which the yeast sinks to the bottom of the tank during fermentation.

BRISKET
Requires long, slow cooking. A cut of beef taken from the breast section under the first five ribs.

BRUNOISE
Finely diced or shredded.

CALAMARI
Squid.

JULIENNE
Foods that are cut into thin, matchstick strips.

MARINADE
A seasoned liquid in which foods are soaked in order to absorb flavour and be tenderized.

MIREPOIX
Diced carrots, onions and celery.

OYSTER SAUCE
A dark brown sauce consisting of oysters, brine and soy sauce cooked until thick and concentrated.

ROUX
A mixture of fat and flour.

SAUTÉ PAN
A wide pan with straight or slightly curved sides that are generally a little higher than those of a frying pan.

SIMMER
To cook food gently in liquid about 185°F.

SOY SAUCE
A dark, salty sauce made by fermenting boiled soy beans and roasted wheat or barley.

STRUDEL DOUGH
Phyllo.

VELOUTÉ
A white stock thickened with a white roux.

I would like to thank the following individuals for their role in the completion of this book:

Chef Brian Abbott

Chef Roger Andrews

Lisa Avery

Chef Gil Bromley

CCFCC - St. John's Branch

Chef Gordon Chalker

Culinary Arts Dept. of The College
of the North Atlantic

Chef Vince Dinillo

Chef Patti Dooley

Paul Forward

Gail Gosse

Anne Hutcheson

Chef Marilyn Lewis

Chef Roary MacPherson

Pat McGuire

Darren Moore

Randy Pike

Joan Rumsey

Chef Angie Ryan

My wife Alice

My fishing buddies Pat, Randy, Darren,
Terry, Richard, Paul and Craig

INDEX